BIRTHSTONES in the PROVINCE of MERCY

Also by Bo Hee Moon

Omma, Sea of Joy and Other Astrological Signs

BIRTHSTONES in the PROVINCE of MERCY

POEMS

Bo Hee Moon

MILKWEED EDITIONS

© 2026, Text by Bo Hee Moon

All rights reserved. No portion of this book may be used or reproduced for the training of artificial intelligence. Except for brief quotations in critical articles or reviews, no part of this book may be reproduced in any manner without prior written permission from the publisher: Milkweed Editions, 1011 Washington Avenue South, Suite 300, Minneapolis, Minnesota 55415. (800) 520-6455

milkweed.org

Published 2026 by Milkweed Editions

Printed in Canada

Cover design by Mary Austin Speaker

Cover artwork by Ran Hwang

Author photo by Christopher Zebo

26 27 28 29 30   5 4 3 2 1

First Edition

Library of Congress Cataloging-in-Publication Data

Names: Moon, Bo Hee author

Title: Birthstones in the province of mercy : poems / Bo Hee Moon.

Description: First edition. | Minneapolis, Minnesota : Milkweed Editions, 2026. | Includes bibliographical references. | Summary: "A collection of poems that confront the complex emotions that accompany understanding identity and belonging after transnational, cross-cultural adoption"-- Provided by publisher.

Identifiers: LCCN 2025024112 (print) | LCCN 2025024113 (ebook) | ISBN 9781571315731 trade paperback | ISBN 9781571311528 ebook

Subjects: LCGFT: Poetry

Classification: LCC PS3619.C4849 B57 2026 (print) | LCC PS3619.C4849 (ebook) | DDC 811/.6--dc23/eng/20250522

LC record available at https://lccn.loc.gov/2025024112

LC ebook record available at https://lccn.loc.gov/2025024113

For you, the reader

CONTENTS

BIRTHSTONES in the PROVINCE of MERCY

DIVINATION/CLOUD

GENEROSITY *GWANDAE* (관대)

My heartspace feels like a bitter fruit,
a meanness, turning to a sweet red-orange.
Hongsi (홍시) is a soft persimmon.
And in another musical city, in the last days
of the year of the metal ox, my heart again feels green.
After I feigned sleep to live through my terror,
after I formed addictions to substitutions,
someone like *omma* lifts my chin, strokes
my cheek. *Chinjeol* (친절) and *dajeong* (다정)
are both words for kindness in Korean.
There is tenderness between strangers
and tenderness between you & those who know you.
When the sky is clouded, when the sky is bright,
two voices melt together in a song,
even when I feel unclear, even if I feel sick.
Hugwang (후광) is like a halo. Some treasures come
unexpectedly—a reunion in the aching and the desire,
a reunion in the fields of roses and wild tea.

Gijesa (기제사): November 10, 1992

On *omma*'s death day,
I forgo the forbidden:

peaches, garlic, red spice—
foods that chase

away spirits. Instead,
there is *dduk guk* (떡국)

and *namul* (나물),
a handful of prairie lilies

and rain lilies that reminds me
of a white summer dress

and where I am—this country
is beautiful, star violet, silver

sage, rabbit tobacco, sweet
pea, yellow water lily, *miguk* (미국)—

I am talking to her at night,
the earliest hour of her death.

The prey outwits
the predator by seeing

the pattern, death & men,
fear & arousal, I bow

deeply twice. When she died,
"How Do You Talk

to An Angel" was the top song,
a whisper of her life, black

seeds in a tiny wildflower.

Omma's Shame

Born in another city,
I left her peninsula,
my birth mother
didn't care for her body—

by the water, we are talking
the same language,

omma and me, *sae* (새)
is "bird." Is it true

that *heundeullineun sang* (흔들리는상)
is "shimmer"? Naturally
stunning, how free we
could feel. I have
my obsession
in my blood. Going
unnoticed by
the Hangang Bridge
(한강대교),
I have the skin
of a poor peasant.
Unable to fix
familiar people,
I return my substitute
father's wedding
band to be melted
down and gone. Lighter
in my spirit, the debt
has been paid.

1963

A fisherman
may have found Kim Ju-yul (김주열)
dead in a South
Korean harbor
a few years
before *omma*
was born, though some say
his body washed
ashore in Masan.
During her birth year,
the Beatles sang,
"I want to hold your
hand." I have
to know—her
offerings on
Chilseok (칠석),

a cucumber
and *a melon*—

how to make
something grow,

how even if she
had not heard about

Valentina Tereshkova
or that the year I was born

a hybrid solar
eclipse lasted

7.57 seconds, it is
as if *omma* knew

certain conditions must
be met for hoarfrost

to be seen on a jam-red
barberry in Moscow.

Like a lamb's blood
on a door, she held me,

barely perceptible
but definite. We cried

immediately for a split second,
knees on nature, kissing

our country, a wild
"honey" *beolkkul* (벌꿀).

Adoption File 1987

Beginning in desire
with half-moons
and *gyungdan* (경단),

a black sesame rice
cake, this night
is for splashing
in water. My first year
was extreme
terror. My papers say

conjunctivitis in Korea,
an upper respiratory
infection in America,
a boy with "extreme
jealousy"—being alive
and unmolested

with the hope
of saying Korean words
right, my heart

responds—a snow crystal
nun gyeoljeong (눈 결정),
light *bich* (빛), a wish *bujeok* (부적)

written in red ink.
My papers say
I said "bye bye

with meaning."
The red spider
lily, the equinox

flower of final
endings and rebirth,
flourishes in my birthplace.

Year of the Black Tiger

On an elvan stone, eggs
become nutty and brown.
Daltokki (달토끼)
is the moon rabbit
who threw himself
into a fire. This year
is for my ancestors. As
sunlight hits some grass,
black is yin like water.
By a street I am on,
I taste *pa* (파)
green onions, Korean
women pick plant
elixirs. As if we are
magnificently bare like clouds
or forest mushrooms,
omma gives me
my life which is as sweet
and maddening as love. We
are sharing—a promise:
white rice cakes in a clear broth—
on our lunar new year, our *Seollal* (설날).

Year of the Yin Black Rabbit

My substitute
father spoke

about his male
infertility.

I read about
the folk charm

of picking
rare fruit

from a pink
tree that has

been dormant.
Apple and apology

sound the same
in Korean,

sagwa (사과).
Where I

used to live,
wild apples

weighed
heavy on

the branches.
My body

recalled
my years

of sadness.
I succumbed

briefly to
the melancholy

of a city
surrounded

by water. In Korea,
women burnt

their fallen hairs
for protection.

Skin and hair
come from one's

ancestors. Nowadays,
I am making

amends
for abandoning

my body. Korean
medicine

says angelica
root stops

the bleeding.
All this

is to say
I have lit incense

for my dead *omma*'s
altar. Warming

my earlobes
with night-

songs, watery
radish kimchi

is for winter.
A boat ritual

is for a baby
with an earache,

a baby who
cannot sleep.

Hours of the Rabbit/Fortune Cookie

From the kitchen
window, he surveyed

the jumping
cottontails.

An eastern cottontail
is generally receptive

for less than a day.
In a lurky place, he claimed

that I should
be grateful. After my substitute

mother quit, I cleaned
his blank tiles.

My DNA traits
were like a paternity test,

proof I was not his.
Subsequently, I had

fixed attachment
points, leaving behind

my legal guardians'
bloodroot

for the natal saplings
and fat of my astral hours.

A Star Nursery

"I'm a legend

in my own mind," he said—
a weakness orbiting

around a lesser
charge. A bond

re-formed
due to spatial

proximity.
Dependent—

my substitute
father pitched a tent.

He urged me
to score—

surface tension.
I called him Papa.

Another father
asked if I was a virgin.

In February, the pool
at my apartment

complex is empty.
An orange

sphere of self-gravity
nears the end

of its luster.
He said adopting me

filled a hole
in his family.

An internal
energy swirls

in a nursery
of brume

and knots,
a baby sling—

metals from a distant
core-collapse.

The Body After Trauma—Desire

Each flashback
has a lesson. M dwarf
stars are smaller,
cooler, fainter
than our Sun
and more active,
explosively active,
→ *intense ultraviolet*
light. Having energy
is the effect
of my sovereignty.
Often getting
my attention,

the sun falls
and rises, markers
to reset, the body
stretching like a sore ankle
in water. Do you ever
catch yourself
creating the same situations?
More than anything
I want to be free
of giving my attention

to the dead stimuli
flickering in my childhood

neural circuitry,
which is why I am looking

into stars and atoms.
M dwarf stars take longer,

longer than the other stars, to form—
slowly, efficiently blazing.

The Body After Trauma—Transformation

To love my body, I do
the practical things—
I notice the scent
of my nature,
my blood rich
with minerals,
my breasts relaxed,
my black hair growing.
My body has
the mountain
and mountain's apples
in her flesh—
the pain of the past
cannot be solved
with a slow dance.
Only a bit taller
than me, his shirt
soft red
flannel against
my cheek,
I do not know him.

I have held out the spoon,
rib sauce on my cheek.
My daily life involves
not remembering
Korean street language
or the thoughts of a poor
woman walking on a dirt
road or what the brain

told my body after
being traumatized & re-
traumatized—I am changing
out of these old clothes,
which requires no effort
or focus, I am changing, completely,
behind a rice paper door.

The Body After Trauma—Innocence

I have been wondering
how to say "rose"
in *omma*'s tongue,
jangmi (장미), what her

radish soup tasted like,
what she noticed

about snow and snow
flowers, *noon ggot* (눈꽃).
I would ask her which
women's names
she liked best, how
to take off
the gold pin that
shows I've been
groomed, if she
watered rapeseed
flowers and barley.
Daeboreum (대보름)
is for the first full
moon of the lunar

year, *fernbrakes, strips*
of pumpkin, a charcoal fire.
Her last full moon
was in the year

of the metal goat,
a hard-boiled egg
for my springtime.

OFFERINGS TO THE SPIRITS/STONE

Feast for the 21st Day

An American couple wrote letters
to an adoption agency. My substitute father

desired a pretty daughter. Two countries
negotiated soft power. My substitute mother

often lied, saying we were "completely bonded,"
wrapping me in a light blue blanket. Before I

became temporarily theirs, I intuited an astonishing
beauty, the fuzzy, bitter leaves beside a girl

on a roadside in a halved country, the dreams
only she could guess in her secret soundscape—

woodsy bulbs of Korean chives, braided rice
straw and pine suspended over a newborn's gate.

What Grows in South Korea

In different times,
"*bogo sipeoyo* (보고 싶어요),"

I whisper to my dead
omma, who was

young in the 80s,
telling her, "I miss you."

Like some other
adopted Korean

girls—my heart
hurts so I stir

up cures. We
were brave, tough

little girls of the rural
Korean peasantry.

I was usually
the secretive friend

who blew out
her birthday

candle, a girl
in a sunhat

running out
of a doorway.

My dictionary
says *yuseong* (유성)

is a "shooting star"—show me (on
the map).

Korean Little Girl—*Eolin Sonyeo* (어린 소녀)

Before you
there was music:

nylon strings,
a woman's wailing,

her hands plucking
a *gayageum* (가야금).

The bluebird
parang sae (파랑새)

is the sky. You are
already free.

"How did you fly
 across miles

of water?"
As the lowest,

ch'ommin (천민)—
there's real

magic in being
a shamanic

ancestor, a seer.
Beware of men

who ask
for a rabbit's liver,

your softness
belongs to you.

There are no more
Siberian tigers in Korea.

Aware of sound—
a calligraphy

brush, a mallet,
a rice ball, a thread

are here for your *doljabi* (돌잡이),
for your choosing.

Birth Hour—How to Name a Child

Like traditional matchmaking,
a rose-honeyed coalescence—some meetings

feel destined, black hair washed
in iris water, an amulet hung above

my door. Reaching for my birth mother,
a future girl has her name picked out, tasting

her white rice cake and dreaming,
unforgotten, in the music of my voice.

"Night" in Korean is not to be confused
with the Korean word for "room."

Did anyone help my birth mother
with the rituals after giving birth?

Whether I held on or came out quickly, I fled
in the night—a pure creek

studded in absolution, or starlight—
women helped me to break the rules

as traditional sweets were offered for her baby's
100th day, as if I can live my life so beautifully,

complete with error and protected from evil,
my birth mother would not regret anything.

Sacrifice: I Was Named by the Orphanage

My singing
voice

is not very
good, my substitute

father said
before my

Torah portion—
he was getting

stoned in
the bathroom,

an air vent
on. Cast out

and drifting
farther from

omma,
I made

my way across
an ocean.

I have always
loved Moses's

story, Jochebed's
baby in

an ark
of bulrushes—

this is the love
of a mother

which I heard
in Sunday

school. I was
raised by

a Jewish family
but only learned

words like *meshuggenah*
and *babushka.*

I am on my own,
and years have passed

since then. After a song
is sung for exorcism,

a basket
is on the floor

for offerings,
rice, spoons,

a candle, and thread—
a Buddhist dance

is not for spectators
but *an offering*

of the dancers'
bodies to

the Buddha.
I tell myself *omma*

had a say
in my name,

my small boat
rocked

against the shores
of her hot desire.

My name is old.
My name

means *jewel girl.*

BFF

Back then when
we both liked

Chinese food
but never talked

about our birth
mothers, I could not

be honest. We met
in Sunday school

where you ate
gefilte fish

which was
before

the synagogue
disintegrated

under the cantor's
prostitution ring.

Remember the time
when I sent you

Bob Dylan song
lyrics and said

we couldn't
be friends?

I am sorry.
You never had

a dog, a confidant
to whisper to

after your substitute
mother suggested

a boob job
or your substitute

father made
sexual comments.

I am reading
about incest

studies—
A woman picks

up the phone, a stranger
asking her—

"Did a family
member touch

you?"—and she
says that it

did not affect
her very much

but resists naming
her father.

Clingy and frightened
my first two weeks

in America
were difficult,

though my adoption
records say

I "got over this,"
and appeared

"emotionally
normal," if I am honest

I would tell you
how scared

I was
because actually

my substitute
father was driving

high on slick
highways,

telling me,
"I would

never hurt
you." And

I would be happy
if you have

a dog now
who kisses

your face
after a good

cry, whose
breathing

calms your own.

Longing for the Family Blessing

As I listened
to an unwed

mother in Naju,
South Korea,

speak, I sobbed.
The women ushered

in watermelon
and rice cakes,

a slender silver
fork before

me. Tenderness
exposed

my longing
to connect

with a musical
voice, a soft

shoe sliding
on a foot,

cool and bare.
Flattering

me, a naked
young woman

who left
the door open—

my substitute
father hugged me

good morning.
I have started asking

myself about
my *minor experiences*

with sexual abuse,
unwanted kisses

and verbal
suggestions.

A hot pink
envelope arrives—

"I've been
dreaming of you

often—flying
over New Mexico,"

my substitute mother writes.
She does not know

about *Korean*
symbols for wishes—

bamboo,
a cloud, stones,

peaches—
a sword dance

for a girl's victory.

Longing for My Birth Father

In a hushed
room, I absorb

a regional
child's song

where a girl
gathers ferns

for her father.
You may have

passed down
your appetites—

eyeing crescent
cakes of red beans

and dates. In my
initial months,

I frowned against
a bright light. I slept lying

on my side or belly. Father:
no record/Mother: no

record/Family
Origin: Hanyang.

I can understand
why you deserted

my birth mother,
though you may

not enter my delicate
space of Korean

water deer
and pale jade

that is solely mine
because as I endured

non-touching abuse
and touching, I witnessed

the starless
parts of human

nature. Alternately,
I am in the village

of the first temple
and tidal flats

where you were once
on business. You are sixty-two.

Bracken
glistens amidst

the yellow soil.
A slender bundle

is in my hands,
a bouquet—

summer green
like my birthstone.

Birth Father *Abeoji* (아버지)—*Invitation to Tea*

It is too soon
to call you *appa* (아빠).

Like a Korean
tea bowl,

my body
was used

as someone
else's treasure.

Grieving in
my sleep,

I saw an older
man like you

recovering
from being

disrespected.
Maybe after calling

each other honey *yubo* (여보),
my birth mother

thought you would
take us to

another country.
Perhaps, when you

married another
woman, there was

a red box
of bridal gifts

and *sajudanja* (사주단자),
a traditional letter

with your birth time.
I am trying

to say that when a man
wrote me, asking

if I was his daughter,
I responded, "What

year was she born?"
When my birth

mother was pregnant,
did she select

an auspicious
name? The

energy of a dead
one's bones

becomes one
with the earth,

your descendant.
Perhaps, you can

tell me where she is.
Today is a charmed

invitation for rice
tea, a tea offering,

shelter for
a kindred traveler.

Dear Birth Father—*Rice Cake Songs*

Omma left me with a desire to know you—a small fortune,
baekseolgi (백설기), a white rice cake, snowdrifts of clouds.

In my fantasies, you remember me and *omma*'s labor pains,
the look on her mother's face after delivery, the path she took home

from the maternity clinic feeling empty-handed,
except you were not there with her. I have sought a decent father.

The rice cake looks bigger in someone else's hand
means that I was left wanting. Do you ever think of me?

A clear bowl of water was placed next to a woman giving birth,
honoring the Birth Grandmother, goddess of children.

Where are you now, birth father? *Sebae* (세배) is a deep bow to elders
on the Lunar New Year. I find you in my heartache—*a rice cake*
in both hands.

Letters to My Half Siblings

Breaking
the wishbone

in my substitute
family

was a tradition.
When I asked

what caused
my birth mother's

death the adoption
agency said

they couldn't
tell me

because my
birth father

may have
living children.

"Half" in Korean
is *ban* (반).

There's half
a moon

and half
a country.

My substitute
brother

pressured
me to eat

rabbit shit.

"Falls asleep

when
carried

on one's back"
is how

I was described
in my records.

A friend
translates:

ibok (이복)
means "different belly/

womb—
different

mother."
Half brother

is *ibokhyeongje* (이복형제).
Half sister

is *ibokjamae* (이복자매).
You know what

our birth father
was like eating salted fish,

his face when
he woke

and drank tea,
how he looked

when he saw you
running toward him,

which women
he may have loved,

the color of his eyes
as he looked out

at the red loess,
the scarred,

yellow earth.

Halmeoni

Facing
the East,

you
and *omma*

knew
the

ancestral
rites

that
feed

the future,
how to

let me go.
Omma

had a
small

frame.
Everything

showed, hills
of green

tea, rain
dissipating

a stuffy
summer—

two separate
loves should

have
been:

Daddy/
my

romantic
partner

/*night*
and *death*

sound
similar

in Japanese.
In our

family,
the women

could not
afford

a dish
dried in

the wind,
gulbi (굴비) dunked

in green
tea. *Borigulbi* (보리굴비)

is said
to restore

the appetite.
A woman your

age said,
When

I returned,
I had a deep

wound.
Another

woman
told her

daughter
to stay

with
the man

who
wounded

her. I have
been scared

of starving.
I have been

celibate.
After years

of smiling
back

at my
captor,

I left
captivity.

Wood
gives

birth
to fire.

I offer
you new

rice
and this

slight
gesture

of turning
my

head
as you

take a
drink.

I think
of you.

Your
daughter

died in
her twenties.

We can
talk

quietly
in strange

tongues
about

which red
fruits our

ancestors
liked best

and if you used
a *binyeo* (비녀)

to hold
up your hair.

Do you
believe in

coincidences?
There were

moments
I imagined

what it
would have

felt like
if I had

one person
in my childhood

who
loved

me while
I drank

from the city's
lake instead of

the rivers
and streams

of our
province. Wishes

bedecked
my hair

like green
jade. I prayed

for the first
leaves, unviolated

and blessed,
after a war-

torn harvest.

EXORCISMS/PEACH

Practice for Living

A poet who loves peaches, melons, and possibly hunger writes
me back: a few words. What's sweeter is that a baby calls
and a mother comes in the early light. Children giving names
to the wild plum bark, to their ghosts, "You can't do anything,"
the child says. Blurry eyes mean a longing for home,
but we're unsure what home means. Google says so.
A friend surprises me with dark chocolate cherries, a poet
shows me her dog in a small fluffy cloud, therefore time
is not what we think. Almost lifting from the body, a woman's soft
brown hair is flying through the woods, we talk of cures and a yellow
bird. Falling into me is the taste of lime, salving laughter. We all want
just a little more time in the presence of what is not yet known,
closer to those who have the hunger, some call it that,
for the sound that is us—the place. her room. our table.

LETTERS TO *OMMA*—*MEETING AT THE MIDPOINT*

사랑해요 *saranghaeyo* (I love you).
Or is it more correct to say
사랑합니다 *saranghamnida*?

감사합니다 *gamsahabnida* (thank you)
for giving me a better life
than I would have had in Korea.

I am aware of the great suffering you endured.
I do not know if this is right: I forgive you.

I sense you want a life for me
where I don't need to use 눈치 *nunchi*
(1. eye-measure; 2. the art of sensing

what people are thinking and feeling).
눈치 있다 *nunchi itda*
is to understand a situation quickly.

I hope you will visit me in my dreams
or the woods or by the sea, our ocean.
Once I saw a painting, *The Wife,*

an elegant dancer, in the Van Gogh Museum,
which I can only somewhat remember now
like a meaningful conversation between a mother

and her baby. Are you trying to tell me
I am catching dead fish with my net? Dropping
the good girl act and accepting the punishment,

I make the choice to back myself as you, 엄마 *omma,*
once did for me. Birth mother—I know what you felt
and that you like salt. 감사합니다 *gamsahabnida* (thank you).

Letters to *Omma*—Attraction

This earthly
cycle you

would be sixty.
Hwangap (환갑)

is the sixtieth
birthday

party. In Korean
traditional

culture, there were
past customs,

the first sound,
first snow,

first light.
Seeing a girl

first thing
on the start

of the year
spelt bad luck.

Boys flew kites.
I admit that

I held onto
my substitute

family. I throw
down a blanket

for us to sit on,
but, of course,

you are not here.
A guest is leaving.

Still, my palms
facing down,

I bow before
you, a celebration,

thimble-sized
rice cakes made

over hot stones.

Letters to *Omma*—Music

During *salpurichum* (살풀이춤),
a ritualistic dance

with a white silk scarf,
musicians improvise a music

called *sinawi* (시나위),
a three-split-beat rhythm.

I feel my black hair, rust-
red leaves, with the ephemeral

body you loved. Untwining
from a harmful ghost,

I was unsupervised
with my caretakers, a roach

on the motel floor.
You probably would have

had me draw what I needed
from your bones, which suggests

you did not have enough
to survive. I have had trouble sleeping.

Traditional percussive music is set
to the rhythm of the breath.

Like the five elements,
the sounds are not separate.

A cloud plate gong
calls to the wandering

and protects the house
from fire. I leave a trail of salt

in the cities I visit. As if tucking
a white star-shaped blossom

behind my ear, there is a way
to find me. As you come nearer,

I pull up my face veil like a dancer
liberating the ghost of my previous

family, joyful tears after
spells of habitual hauntings.

Letters to *Omma*—Escape

If this is our final goodbye,
after I sponge you

and bathe you
in sandalwood water,

let me take your hand
and clip your fingernails,

gathering the clippings
of you into small bags.

Into a quilt that cushions
your body, I have sewn

travel money
for the other world.

I wrap hemp around you
like your chrysalis,

free of knots
and entanglements.

Outside my front door
a lantern hangs.

I am shy. Actually,
are you returning

to earth as white butterflies
to say goodbye? I search

for you everyplace, but I only
have my birth chart

to go off of and this tiny,
careful body you gave me.

I hope when I die,
my body is cleansed

of mistakes, a luxury
you did not have.

Bury me simply.
Reaching the sea

is my recurring dream.
Close to you,

I do not shoo
away the butterflies.

After failing
many times, I remove

obstructions, which is
how I know I am flying.

A kite is cut from its bobbin,
a butterfly dance.

Letters to *Omma*—Reunion

Wild Korean
ginseng

needs to remain
untouched

for years,
growing

in the mountains,
long roots

like witchy hair.
On a flight

across continents,
I was yanked

from my country
and later fed soymilk

formula. Placed in
the arms

of my substitute
father, who

mistook
my affection

for consent.
He called me

his "date."
Like a sick joke

I developed
early

as some
girls do

in predatory
families. "Daughters

marry their fathers,"
he said, grinning,

and named
my future baby Epiphany.

He consumed
whatever he

wanted, his
speech

around me
like an arm

in the one-dollar movie
theater. But

he does not know
my new address. My nature

is of my
birth mother.

I comfort a girl
crying quietly

in a bathroom
stall. Renewing

the earth, water
moves across rice

paddies and clover—
scarring forms

on the taproot
of ginseng

with each year's
new leaves.

The bitter red
fruit attracts

wood thrushes
where I live now—

a sudden spring
pea, eastern

pink light,
budding gently

before me.
My birth

mother was
not nameless.

She had a scent,
a sound.

I wonder
if she visited

the spirit mothers,
yeo-sanshin, of the Korean

mountains
and prayed

for a child
and for the rain,

for my birth
father to be other

than he was.
If I could

meet my birth
mother again,

I would begin by
looking into her eyes,

a fragile depth
between us,

black loam
for my tender roots.

LETTERS TO *OMMA*—HOW YOU MET

Since I do not know
exactly how you met,

let me envision it.
In April, Korean azaleas

peek through.
Flower rice cakes

hwajeon (화전)
are pressed.

I've been told
a story—

you met at a picnic.
Burning the banks

of rice paddies
made way

for new growth,
his name and your name

spoken, honeyed
and finished

with salt. I have
been collecting

the names of melodies,
rice in aster leaves.

During a folk tradition,
villagers held hands

for prayers
in the cold night.

You could have
stood close

to your mother,
yearning for your lover

to be good to you,
for the humidity

to cease, for an
original hymn

to call your own,
a wild violet

in the flowering
mountain ash.

Letters to *Omma*—Ceremony of Mercy

A brush dipped
into an unrushed

freedom, I consider
how calligraphy

can reveal
a person's character.

I have been hard
on myself,

seeking your
essence

at the core
of my deepest

wish—a rain
rite, a layered

rice cake, a prayer
at sunrise. In Korean

folklore, a fire dog
bites the moon,

a lunar eclipse.
The dog drops

the moon. I cannot
hold you

because you do not
want to be held.

I am mortal,
and my seeking

has formed
a zigzagged path.

Mercy is the dog
coming back

after not succeeding,
a loyal companion

in the burnt
pine and dawn.

Letters to *Omma*—*Expelling the Nocturnal Ghosts*

The edge of an iris,
a hairpin, releases

an adult woman's
black waves—

I press my thighs
together. Tight

chest, I fall for a man,
birth root,

and envy those with fathers.
First slivers

of my secret
desire—your peppery

heat is in my cry.
During the second

lunar month, a glowing,
nocturnal ghost stole

a child's shoes.
Seasons later,

my birth father
cannot replant

my seedlings in June's
rice paddies. Uncontrollable

as my birth father
and you happening

upon each other, lux
tied to hearing the hard bark

or rasp of *the first animal*
sound, I bare my neck,

strawberry
birthmark, your young

motherwort
and moss-rose

in soil like a persimmon
in brown sugar, a bitter *rice nectar*—

a verdant birthnight
after the monsoons.

NOTES

Some of the poems in this collection include and alter language from the following books: Yoon Seo-seok, *Festive Occasions: The Customs in Korea,* trans. Cho Yoon-jung and Park Hyun-ju (Ewha Womans University Press, 2008); The National Academy of the Korean Language, *An Illustrated Guide to Korean Culture: 233 Traditional Key Words* (Hakgojae, 2002); The National Folk Museum of Korea, *Encyclopedia of Korean Folk Beliefs: Encyclopedia of Korean Folklore and Traditional Culture Vol. II* (National Folk Museum of Korea, 2013); The National Folk Museum of Korea, *Encyclopedia of Korean Folk Literature: Encyclopedia of Korean Folklore and Traditional Culture Vol. III* (National Folk Museum of Korea, 2014); and The National Folk Museum of Korea, *Encyclopedia of Korean Seasonal Customs: Encyclopedia of Korean Folklore and Traditional Culture Vol. I* (National Folk Museum of Korea, 2010).

Year of the Black Tiger

This poem includes a reference to *Daltokki* (달토끼): "The Moon Rabbit (Daltokki, 달토끼)," *Gwangju News,* September 29, 2017, https://gwangjunewsgic.com/arts-culture/korean-culture/daltokki/. According to this article, the rabbit is an important symbol during Chuseok and appears in the retelling of a Korean folktale: "Ashamed at his feeble offering, the rabbit, in an act of self-sacrifice, proceeded to ignite the grass he'd gathered and threw himself into the flames to be eaten by the beggar as a meal. The action of the rabbit so touched the beggar-emperor that he placed the rabbit in the moon to become its guardian and surrounded him with smoke as a reminder to all of the rabbit's noble death."

Year of the Yin Black Rabbit

This poem includes and alters language from Takashi Akiba, "A Study on Korean Folkways," *Folklore Studies* 16 (1957): i–106, https://doi.org/10.2307/1177360; and Na-Young Choi, "Symbolism of Hairstyles in Korea and Japan," *Asian Folklore Studies* 65, no. 1 (2006): 69–86, http://www.jstor.org/stable/30030374.

The Body After Trauma—Desire

This poem includes phrases from Bill Steigerwald and Nancy Jones, "New Technique May Give NASA's Webb Telescope a Way to Quickly Identify Planets with Oxygen," NASA, January 6, 2020, https://exoplanets.nasa.gov/news/1615/new-technique-may-give-nasas-webb-telescope-a-way-to-quickly-identify-planets-with-oxygen.

Feast for the 21st Day

This poem includes and alters language from Eleana Kim, "The Origins of Korean Adoption: Cold War Geopolitics and Intimate Diplomacy," *UC Irvine*, 2009, https://escholarship.org/uc/item/78q9q34d. Its title comes from Yoon Seo-seok, *Festive Occasions: The Customs in Korea*, trans. Cho Yoon-jung and Park Hyun-ju, (Ewha Womans University Press, 2008): "The baby's well-being is celebrated 21 days after birth."

Korean Little Girl—*Eolin Sonyeo* (어린 소녀)
This poem includes and alters language from the following: Eunjung Choi and Sumi Kwon, "Multicultural Approach to Korean Contemporary Music with the Traditional Folk Song 'Bird, Bird, Blue Bird,'" *American Music Teacher* 62, no. 4 (February/March 2013): https://www.jstor.org/stable/i40140701; Sangmi Kang, "Sharing Global Musics: Bring Korea's 'Arirang' to Your Music Class," *Music Educators Journal* 100, no. 1 (September 2013): 32–35, https://doi.org/10.1177/0027432113495514; and Otojit Kshetrimayum, "Women and Shamanism in Manipur and Korea: A Comparative Study," *Indian Anthropologist* 39, no. 1/2 (2009): 17–34, https://www.jstor.org/stable/41920088.

Sacrifice: I Was Named by the Orphanage
This poem includes and alters language from Man-young Hahn, "The Four Musical Types of Buddhist Chant in Korea," *Yearbook for Traditional Music* 15, (1983): 45–58, https://doi.org/10.2307/768641.

Longing for the Family Blessing
This poem includes and alters language from Diana E. H. Russell, *The Secret Trauma: Incest in the Lives of Girls and Women* (Basic Books, 1987) and Sookmyung Women's University Museum, "Longing for the Family Blessing," *Korean Symbols of Wishes,* https://artsandculture.google.com/story/korean-symbols-of-wishes-sookmyung-women%E2%80%99s-university-museum/EAWhwWOcljD-IA?hl=en, from which it also takes its title. The poem is informed by Judy van Zile, "*Chinju Kommu*: An Implement Dance of Korea," *Studia Musicologica Academiae Scientarium Hungaricae* 33, no. 1/4 (1991): 359–66, https://doi.org/10.2307/902458.

Longing for My Birth Father

This poem includes and alters language from Lee E-Wha, *Korea's Pastimes and Customs: A Social History,* trans. Ju-Hee Park (Homa & Sekey Books, 2005).

I gained inspiration from Jennifer Kwon Dobbs, "Fact Sheet," *Paper Pavilion* (White Pine Press, 2007).

Birth Father *Abeoji* (아버지)—*Invitation to Tea*

This poem includes and adapts language from Andrew Eungi Kim, "Nonofficial Religion in South Korea: Prevalence of Fortunetelling and Other Forms of Divination," *Review of Religious Research* 46, no. 3 (March 2005): 284–302, https://doi.org/10.2307/3512557.

This poem is also informed by and includes language from National Folk Museum of Korea, *The Life of a Korean: The 4 Ceremonies of a "Yangban" Joseon Dynasty Nobleman,* https://artsandculture.google.com/story/the-life-of-a-korean-national-folk-museum-of-korea/7AVhSBrQx0lzKA?hl=en.

Halmeoni

The poem includes a quote from Josh Smith and Haejin Choi, "South Korea's Surviving 'Comfort Women' Spend Final Years Seeking Atonement from Japan," *Reuters,* December 19, 2018, https://www.reuters.com/article/world/south-koreas-surviving-comfort-women-spend-final-years-seeking-atonement-from-idUSKBN1OI0BU/. In this article, Lee Yong-soo says, "When I returned, I had a deep wound."

The poem also includes and alters language from the following: Alle Blessing Ovase, "Showing Respect in Korean and Yoruba Cultures," *Korea.net*, December 17, 2019, https://www.korea.net/NewsFocus/HonoraryReporters/view?articleId=180693; Im Eun-byel, "[Epicurean Challenge] Sea Breeze, Barley Heap and Green Tea Water Cook Up Borigulbi," *The Korea Herald*, August 30, 2018, https://www.koreaherald.com/article/1769637; Chang Hyeon Lee, Young Kim, Yang Suk Kim, and Young Yun, "Ancestral Ritual Food of Korean *Jongka*: Historical Changes of the Table Setting," *Journal of Ethnic Foods* 5, no. 2 (June 2018): 121–132, https://doi.org/10.1016/j.jef.2018.06.001; and Dong Zhongshu, "An Official Response Regarding the Five Phases," ed. and trans. Sarah A. Queen and John S. Major, *Luxuriant Gems of the Spring and Autumn* (Columbia University Press, 2016).

Letters to *Omma—Meeting at the Midpoint*
This poem includes and alters language from Euny Hong, "The Korean Secret to Happiness and Success," *The New York Times*, November 2, 2019, https://www.nytimes.com/2019/11/02/opinion/sunday/nunchi.html.

Letters to *Omma*—Music
This poem refers to a traditional Korean dance called *salpurichum*. According to Ohio State University, the dance is a kind of purification: "Traditionally, Koreans believe the souls of the departed must be cleansed of their earthly attachments ahead of their journeys to the other world."

This poem also includes and alters language from Eun-Joo Lee and Yong-Shin Kim, *Salpuri-Chum, A Korean Dance for Expelling Evil Spirits: A Psychoanalytic Interpretation of its Artistic Characteristics* (Hamilton Books, 2017).

Letters to *Omma*—Escape

This poem includes and alters language from the following: Sookja Cho, "Transformation and Deification: Butterflies, Souls, and Cross-Cultural Incarnations," *Transforming Gender and Emotion: The Butterfly Lovers Story in China and Korea* (University of Michigan Press, 2018); Lee Kwang Kyu, "The Concept of Ancestors and Ancestor Worship in Korea," *Asian Folklore Studies* 43, no. 2 (1984): 199–214, https://doi.org/10.2307/1178009; and Kwang-Kyu Lee, "The Practice of Traditional Family Rituals in Contemporary Urban Korea," *Journal of Ritual Studies* 3, no. 2 (Summer 1989): 167–83, https://www.jstor.org/stable/44368935.

Letters to *Omma*—Reunion

This poem includes and alters language from the Indiana Department of Natural Resources's website and James Huntley Grayson, "Female Mountain Spirits in Korea: A Neglected Tradition," *Asian Folklore Studies* 55, no. 1 (1996): 119–34, https://doi.org/10.2307/1178859.

ACKNOWLEDGMENTS

Thank you to the editors of the following journals in which these poems first appeared, sometimes in a different form.

AGNI: "Letters to *Omma*—Reunion"
Copper Nickel: "Letters to *Omma*—How You Met" and "Longing for My Birth Father"
Cream City Review: "Generosity *Gwandae* (관대)" and "Korean Little Girl: *Eolin Sonyeo* (어린 소녀)"
Gulf Coast: "Adoption File 1987"
Pinch: "Letters to *Omma—Expelling the Nocturnal Ghosts*"
Poetry: "Sacrifice: I Was Named by the Orphanage"
Poetry Northwest: "Letters to *Omma*—Ceremony of Mercy"
Radar Poetry: "What Grows in South Korea"
Salt Hill Journal: "The Body After Trauma—Innocence"
So to Speak: "BFF" and "Year of the Black Tiger"
swamp pink: "Birth Father 아버지 (*abeoji*): *Invitation to Tea*" and "Year of the Yin Black Rabbit"
Sweet Tree Review: "Letters to *Omma—Meeting at the Midpoint*" and "Practice for Living"
The Margins: "*Gijesa* (기제사): November 10, 1992"
Tupelo Quarterly: "1963" and "*Omma*'s Shame"
Zone 3: "The Body After Trauma—Desire" and "The Body After Trauma—Transformation"

Thank you to Matthew Olzmann for selecting my collection for the Jake Adam York Prize. I treasure your generous and kind words and your powerful poetry. I am deeply thankful to Wayne Miller and the editors at *Copper Nickel*, including Joanna Luloff, Brian Barker, and Nicky Beer. I appreciate the screeners and all who make this award possible.

A heartfelt thanks to the incredible Daniel Slager and the amazing team at Milkweed Editions, including Sean Beckford, Lauren Langston Klein, Morgan LaRocca, Natalie Wollenzien, and Morissa Young. Thank you to Caron Fasching-Oty for your support and insight with copyedits. Thank you to Mary Austin Speaker for your beautiful book designs and covers.

I am thankful for the University of Houston's Creative Writing and Literature program. Thank you to the brilliant community, including Sarah Ehlers, Jamie H. Ferguson, Nick Flynn, francine j. harris, Antonya Nelson, Alexander Parsons, Kaitlin Rizzo, and spectacular classmates and friends in the program. A special thanks to Erin Belieu, Jason Berger, Kevin Prufer, Martha Serpas, Michael D. Snediker, and Roberto Tejada for warmly welcoming me into the program, nurturing a beautiful community, and encouraging me with my writing. I am immensely thankful for your gifts of kindness, knowledge, and generosity. Thank you to Niki Herd for selecting "Letters to *Omma*—Reunion" for the University of Houston's Academy of American Poets Award.

Many thanks to Rich Levy, Krupa Parikh, and Inprint for your generosity. Thank you to Jonathan Yi, the Jonathan Yi Memorial Scholarship, and the Korean American Scholarship Foundation for your kindness, commitment to supporting the Korean American community, and generous support.

I am extremely grateful for encouragement from fantastic poets and writers. Thank you to Li-Young Lee for your support and remarkable poetry. To Laura Gray-Rosendale for being a brilliant light. To Alison Hawthorne Deming for your magnificent teaching. To Nicole Walker for your kind, generous support. To Matthew Zapruder for being a transformative poet, writer, and teacher, and for being an inspiration. To Lee Herrick, Su Hwang, and Sun Yung Shin for your exquisite radiance. Thank you also to Lee Herrick and Jennifer Kwon Dobbs, along with William Pierce and Shuchi Saraswat, for including my poem, "Letters to *Omma*—Reunion," in *Afterlives: An AGNI Portfolio of Asian Adoptee Diaspora Writing.*

Thank you to friends and community across the country and world. Thank you to Amanda Johnston, Sasha West, and the phenomenal women of the LLL in Austin, Texas. Thank you to Dalia Azim and the Texas Book Festival. Thank you to the Writers' League of Texas. A warm thanks to Patty Prado for your leadership, inspiring presence, and friendship. Deepest gratitude to I.K. for your incredible beauty, compassion, and wisdom. Thank you to Chaeun Moon for your friendship and support. Thank you to the adoptee community. Thank you to S.S. for your powerful love, friendship, and brilliance, which are precious gifts I hold dear. Thank you to my birth mother, birth father, and birth family. Thank you to you, the reader.

A South Korean adoptee, **BO HEE MOON** is the author of one previous book of poems, *Omma, Sea of Joy and Other Astrological Signs*. Her poems have appeared in *AGNI, Poetry, Poetry Northwest, swamp pink, The Margins,* and other journals. She is a PhD student in Literature and Creative Writing at the University of Houston, where she has received the Inprint Brown Foundation Fellowship. Moon currently lives in Houston, and you can find her at boheemoon.com.

The Jake Adam York Prize for a first or second collection of poems was established in 2016 to honor the name and legacy of Jake Adam York (1972–2012). York was the founder of Copper Nickel, a nationally distributed literary journal at the University of Colorado Denver. His work as a poet and scholar explored memory and social history, and particularly the Civil Rights Movement.

The judge for the 2024–25 Jake Adam York Prize was Matthew Olzmann.

Founded as a nonprofit organization in 1980, Milkweed Editions is an independent publisher. Our mission is to identify, nurture, and publish transformative literature, and build an engaged community around it.

We are based in Bde Óta Othúŋwe (Minneapolis) in Mní Sota Makhóčhe (Minnesota), the traditional homeland of the Dakhóta and Anishinaabe (Ojibwe) people and current home to many thousands of Dakhóta, Ojibwe, and other Indigenous people, including four federally recognized Dakhóta nations and seven federally recognized Ojibwe nations.

We believe all flourishing is mutual, and we envision a future in which all can thrive. Realizing such a vision requires reflection on historical legacies and engagement with current realities. We humbly encourage readers to do the same.

milkweed.org

Milkweed Editions, an independent nonprofit literary publisher, gratefully acknowledges sustaining support from our board of directors, the McKnight Foundation, the National Endowment for the Arts, and many generous contributions from foundations, corporations, and thousands of individuals—our readers. This activity is made possible by the voters of Minnesota through a Minnesota State Arts Board Operating Support grant, thanks to a legislative appropriation from the Arts and Cultural Heritage Fund.

Interior design by Mike Corrao
Typeset in Arno Pro

Arno Pro was created by Robert Slimbach in 2007 for the Adobe Originals Program. His design was inspired by the Venetian styles of the 15th and 16th century.

Milkweed Editions is committed to ecological stewardship. We strive to align our operations accordingly and to reduce their environmental impact. We are a member of the Green Press Initiative, a nonprofit coalition of publishers, manufacturers, and authors working to protect the world's endangered forests and conserve natural resources. *Birthstones in the Province of Mercy* was printed on acid-free 100% postconsumer-waste paper by Friesens Corporation.